MY NANA W
FREE-RANGE KID

By Nancy Peek Youngdahl

Outskirts Press, Inc.
http://www.outskirtspress.com

Paperback ISBN: 978-1-4787-0521-5
Hardback ISBN: 978-1-4787-0492-8

Library of Congress Control Number: 2017913915

Illustrated by: Victor Guiza.
Illustrations © 2018 Outskirts Press, Inc.. All rights reserved - used with permission.

Outskirts Press and the "OP" logo are trademarks belonging to Outskirts Press, Inc.

PRINTED IN THE UNITED STATES OF AMERICA

Dedicated to my family
so storytelling and memories
will remain throughout
all of our future generations.

My great-grandmother and great-grandpa are very old. I call my great-grandmother Nana because that's what my mama calls her. She is smart for an old person. When she talks and uses funny words like "gosh darn" or "yawl," it makes me laugh. My granddad, Pops, teases her about saying "burfday" or "goff," instead of "birthday" and "golf." Mama says she talks like this because she is from the South and that's how southern people talk.

My name is Adalee and I am eight years old. My little brother, Henry, is six years old. My great-grandparents make my day bright and I wake up excited for another fun day. My little brother and I love them and we know they love us. If you have great-grandparents, you are lucky too.

SEATTLE

RALEIGH

My great-grandparents live in North Carolina, which is far away from us, but they come to visit pretty often. They have to fly in an airplane to get here. Mama said someday they won't be able to do this anymore. This made me really sad.

We live in Washington State in a house with our mama's parents, who we call Mimi and Pops. Washington State is where lots of big trees grow, and there's a huge mountain called Mount Rainier that has snow on it all year long.

Mimi is beautiful and always has a smile on her face. She is a schoolteacher for big kids.

And Pops builds furniture for lots of people, so they both are very busy doing things that keep them away from home during the day. They don't get to play with us very often, but Nana and my great-grandpa, Skip, always have time. That's because they don't have to work anymore.

M ama keeps a framed picture of my great-grandparents on my bedside table so Henry and I won't forget what they look like when they go back to their home in North Carolina.

⭐ Find the framed picture.

My Nana likes to read to Henry and me, and she tells us stories about when she was a little girl long ago.

Nana told us a story about when she was about our age, a big circus came to her town in the fall and put up huge tents in the field next to their home. The circus arrived each fall in long train cars that held all the animals, the circus people, and the equipment they needed to put up the tents. She guessed the circus was put up in the field next to her home because the train tracks were right across the road.

Nana and her brother, Douglas, loved to go visit with the circus people and watch them put up the tall tents and practice their acts and take care of all the circus animals like elephants, horses, bears and lions. She loved watching the girls in the pretty costumes jump around from swing to swing and hang by their legs.

One year, after Nana and Douglas had spent all day walking around the circus, a man gave them free tickets so they could come back at night to watch the real show. Nana said she planned to run away and join the circus when she grew up! Of course she never did that.

The swings were hung from the tops of the tents and the ladies dangled high up in the air. It scared Nana to watch, but the pretty ladies never fell. Nana and her brother saw lots of clowns with big red noses and colorful baggy clothes and huge floppy feet. The clowns would honk their big red noses and ride around in a tiny car. Nana said the clowns always pretended they were falling down.

After the circus tents were pulled down and the circus people and animals left town on the train, Nana and Douglas decided to have their own circus.

They climbed tall trees in their yard and hung from branches by their legs, even jumping from tree limb to tree limb. Nana said we should never do that because it was very dangerous.

Nana said she fell down on the ground once and had the breath knocked out of her. I didn't know what that meant, but she explained that she couldn't catch her breath, so her brother breathed into her mouth until she felt better.

They also wanted to pretend to be a lion tamer, so they built a tall platform using big rocks and some boards. Nana sat on a chair and pretended to be a lion while Douglas was the lion tamer, holding a long stick.

Nana fell down from the wobbly boards and chair, again knocking the breath out of her. Douglas pulled her by her arms and dragged her into the house and then called their mother to help.

Their mama was sleeping since she had just come home from work and was very tired. Instead of being afraid for her daughter, Nana's mother was angry! Nana and Douglas both got a "spankin" for waking her up.

Nana said they had a cat named Tom, even though it was a girl cat. She didn't know why they named her Tom, but all the cats they ever had were named Tom. Tom was black with white spots. She was a lazy, fat cat that lived in their house and kept the mice away. One day Tom disappeared for a long, long time. Nana and Douglas hunted for Tom, but they couldn't find her. They didn't see her for three months, and then one day she showed up at their back door. Tom was hurt with lots of scratches and cuts and was super skinny. Tom could hardly walk! Nana said she took good care of her, and before long Tom was a fat and happy cat again.

Nana told us that she and Douglas loved to play outside together while their older sister, Barbara, liked to stay inside and read. I agree with Nana; playing outside is much more fun! They lived near woods, and Nana and Douglas liked to pretend they were camping out like they had seen gypsies do.

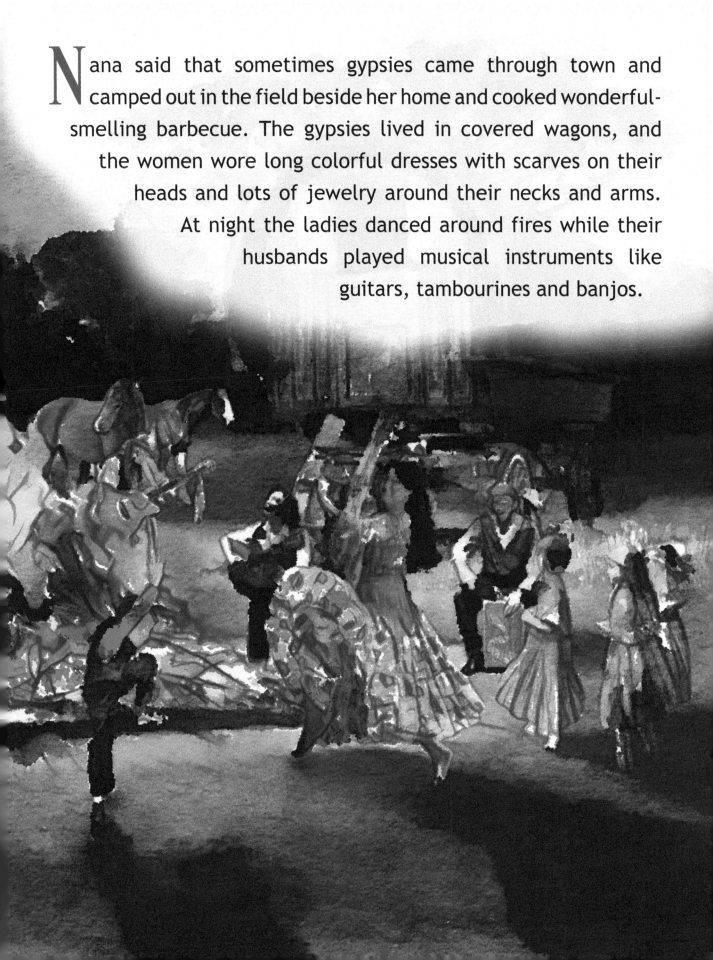

Nana said that sometimes gypsies came through town and camped out in the field beside her home and cooked wonderful-smelling barbecue. The gypsies lived in covered wagons, and the women wore long colorful dresses with scarves on their heads and lots of jewelry around their necks and arms. At night the ladies danced around fires while their husbands played musical instruments like guitars, tambourines and banjos.

One day when Nana and her brother were heading out to the woods to play, they took some matches from home and built a small fire and roasted marshmallows. They took along a jug of water to put the fire out, but after they left the woods, they smelled smoke and looked back to see a big fire.

They ran home and woke their mama and told her they had seen a bunch of gypsies in the woods. This was a big lie, but their mama didn't ask them any more about it.

Their mama was too busy trying to keep the fire from spreading to their backyard by hitting the flames with wet towels! The fire alarm blared throughout the town to alert all of the volunteer firemen to come help put out the fire. Lots of fire trucks came, and the volunteer firemen finally got the fire out, but the whole woods burned down. It took many years for the trees to grow back tall again. No one in Nana's family ever mentioned the fire again. Nana said she and Douglas learned a big lesson: to never play with matches.

Both of Nana's parents had to work, so during the summer the kids stayed home alone. The whole summer they never wore shoes and they ran around barefoot. They lived in the country and their nearest neighbor was a boy named Kenny, who lived half a mile away. Once in a while they walked to see Kenny. Kenny was the same age as Nana and liked to pretend he was in a parade. Nana and her brother would march around and pretend to have musical instruments while Kenny pretended he was the drum major. He carried a big long stick and led them around. Nana said when Kenny grew up and went away to college; he became a real drum major!

Another thing they liked to do with Kenny was lay on his back screened-in porch in the afternoons and read lots of comic books about cowboys and Indians. They also listened to radio stories about the Lone Ranger, his horse Silver, and Tonto, his Indian sidekick. I had never heard of the Lone Ranger before, but Nana explained it to us. Most homes did not have television sets back then, so radios were popular and every home had one.

Nana said when she was little, they didn't have washing machines and dryers like they do today. Saturdays were always washday, and she and Barbara helped her mother fill two big tubs with water. Then they filled the washer, which had a wringer on it, with hot water. Nana's mama would feed the clothes through the wringer to get most of the water out before the clean clothes were put into the tubs that were filled with clean cold water. One time Barbara got her hand caught in the wringer. It hurt, and her hand swelled up for a while, but she was okay.

Their mother hung the clothes outside on rope clotheslines that she had strung between big trees in the backyard so the clothes could dry in the sun. One time during an unexpected storm, Nana said the wind broke the clothesline and all the clothes fell on the ground and got dirty. They had to be rinsed again! Nana says she remembers feeling sad for her mama because she worked so hard all the time.

The hardest part of laundry day was when they had to empty the big tubs and then refill them with clean water. The hot water in the washer was never changed between loads of clothes, so by the time they washed the last load, the water was black! Nana said her mama always washed the white clothes and bedsheets first and the dirtiest clothes, like her dad's greasy work clothes, last.

In the winter or on rainy Saturdays, they hung the clothes up on lines in the living room. That was sort of fun, because Nana and her brother and sister played hide-and-seek among the hanging clothes. Nana said that one very cold and icy Saturday, they hung the clothes outside because the sun was out. However by the end of the day, her daddy's work pants were frozen stiff and looked like he was still wearing them!

Nana said one morning she decided she didn't want to go to school, so she pretended she was sick and stayed home alone. She sat on the couch all day in front of a window and watched to see if anyone was coming to their house. I guess back then, if you weren't in school, people came looking for you. She just knew someone from the school would come to get her and she would be in big trouble. Nana said it was a miserable day and she never did that again.

Nana is always telling us funny stories like these, and we love hearing them. Maybe someday I'll tell you more stories Nana told us. Those old days of long ago were really weird, and I'm glad I live now.

THE END

CPSIA information can be obtained
at www.ICGtesting.com
Printed in the USA
LVHW070911140419
614044LV00001BA/4/P